Living Single God's Way

A Single Woman's Guide to Wholeness

Pastor
Laytecia McKinney

Unless otherwise indicated, all scripture quotations in this volume are from the King James or Amplified Version of the Bible.

First Printing 2016
Copyright @ 2016
By Wisdom in Print Publishing Company
All Rights Reserved
Printed In USA

For Additional copies write to:
Wisdom in Print Publishing Company
c/o Victory Temple Outreach Ministries, Inc.
5819 N. 56th Street
Tampa, FL 33610

WWW.MYVICTORYTEMPLE.ORG

DEDICATION

In loving memory of my beautiful mother, Prophetess *Dorothy L. Brooks,* who exemplified, through her walk with Christ, such strength, integrity and sanctification. You were my hero, my greatest supporter and a true example of a Single Virtuous Christian Woman!

To my loving and beautiful daughter, *Brittany* who is the apple of my eye. My prayer is that the lifestyle that I live before you is a true example of holiness.

To my beloved sisters, *Edwina, Shaneka, Ebony* and *Qquani.* You are "Women of Excellence" who have always been by my side and from whom I can draw strength in my times of weakness. "YOU ARE WHO GOD SAYS THAT YOU ARE".

To my loving son, Dan, you are my inspiration!

ACKNOWLEDGEMENTS

To *Jehovah Jireh* who has provided me with the wisdom, knowledge and passion to write this book. To you Lord, be all glory, majesty, dominion and power, both now and forevermore!

To my husband, Sedrick for being my inspiration and motivation to take what I wrote on paper back in the 1990's and publish it in 2016. It's never too late!

To the Women of Victory Temple, I love you and thanks a million for all of your support, motivation and encouragement! Extra thanks to Evangelist Yolanda Lee-George for all your help to make this dream a reality.

To Elder Annie Atkins for your editing skills, mentorship and motherly love shown to me over the years!

To my Spiritual parents, Apostle Mark T. Jones and Lady Lisa Jones for your covering, godly wisdom and instruction that keeps me balanced and grounded.

FOREWARD

Manifestations Worldwide Inc.

"Living Single God's Way" will serve to be a literary blueprint for perfecting one's own wholeness, while allowing God to integrate the right companion into one's life.

This publication will give you the keys to navigating the treacherous waters of love, dating, and crafting lifelong relationships.

Dr. Mark T. Jones Sr.
Apostle | Author
Manifestations Worldwide Inc.

www.centerformanifestation.com | 3102 E. Lake Ave | Tampa, FL | 33615 |

About the Author

The story and life of Pastor Laytecia Brooks-McKinney is both astounding and illustrating in how hard work and determination in our society can overcome obstacles. Although she yields from ancestry which was not replete with royal pedigree or vast wealth, her diligence and obedience has opened supernatural doors far beyond what our natural eyes could ever envision.

Imbued with humbleness, meekness, intellect and a sense of social and spiritual responsibility, she has long been an advocate to bring healing, restoration, truth and deliverance to the wounded, broken and lost. Not one to merely rest on the laurels of her predecessors in her growth and walk with Christ, she earned several degrees graduating with honors during her matriculation. Her exemplary standards and genuine love for God's people resonates the very meaning of the adage that, "the will of God will never take you where the Grace of God will not celebrate and keep you.

She is the Founder and Senior Pastor of Victory Temple Outreach Ministries, Inc. founded in 2006. She is married to Sedrick and has three children, Brittany, Danielar and stepson, Jermaine and a precious grandson, Amauri. She is an honor graduate of

Hillsborough Community College and Tampa Bay Legal Academy. Always diligent in her commitment to God and education she continued her matriculation at Tampa Bible College where she earned her Masters of Divinity and Christian Counseling Degree.

She was recognized by the City of Tampa in 1996, as a "Woman of Zion" and again in February 2007, as the recipient of the "2007 Employee Black History Award." She has been appointed to preach the gospel and evangelize since the year of 1990. Through her philanthropic services, the WOW Ministries, Inc. (Women of Wisdom) was birthed. She was nominated by On Que Magazine as the 2013 "Female Pastor of the Year for the City of Tampa". Pastor McKinney loves people and has a passion for Christ to see lives changed through the gospel of Jesus Christ.

Living Single God's Way
A Single Woman's Guide to Wholeness

TABLE OF CONTENS

1. Chapter 1:   Single Means to be Whole............1
2. Chapter 2:   Identity Crises...........................16
3. Chapter 3:   The Make-Up of A Woman..........26
4. Chapter 4:   Desiring But Not Desperate........31
5. Chapter 5:   Putting Flesh Under Subjection..48
6. Chapter 6:   The Dating Game......................61
7. Chapter 7:   Rules & Guidelines to Dating......69
8. Chapter 8:   While You Are Waiting...............74

INTRODUCTION

Growing up as young girls playing with Barbie and Ken, we all fantasized about having the perfect mate and the perfect marriage. It was almost every girls dream to grow up, get married and live happily ever after. Well, in reality, it does not always work out the way we dreamed it to be. For centuries we have always put a time clock on women, when they should get married and when they should have children but the Lord's ways are not our ways nor does he move according to our timetable.

If you have reached the expiration date of your, so-called biological clock, hold on my sister for the Lord's ways are past finding out! Many women feel incomplete without having a man in their lives and fall into the spirit of oppression and even depression especially when they have not gotten married or have not had children by a certain age. We have so many clouds of witnesses in the bible letting us know that age has nothing to do with us missing out on what God has promised us.

In the book of Genesis we read that Abraham was seventy-five years old when God promised him and his wife Sarah that they would be the father and mother of many nations and that their seed would be blessed.

The problem was that they had no seed! What God had promised seemed almost impossible to them because Abraham and Sarah were well stricken in age and Sarah's womb had been barren all her life. How many of you know that God can bring life to any dead situation! Twenty-five years later God's promise was fulfilled to them and they gave birth to Isaac, "Son of the Promise". Sometimes your blessing is delayed but it's not denied. The Lord is faithful unto them that wait on him and in His own time He will faithfully bring what He has promised to pass. The Lord wants us to understand that He has the power to accomplish what He has promised only if we just believe and have patience enough to wait on Him.

Philippians 4:11
Not that I speak in respect of want; for I have learned, in whatsoever state I am, therewith to be content.

Chapter 1

SINGLE MEANS TO BE WHOLE

Acts 9:34
....Jesus Christ maketh thee whole, arise and make thy bed.

SINGLE

The word "*Single*" means to be one and one only for one person of the unmarried state, to be a complete whole. Being single means to be complete and to be confident in the Lord and in yourself. It means, not to lack in any area of your life! Being single does not mean that you are alone, Jesus said in *Matthew 28:20..."Lo, I am with you always, even unto the end of the world"*. Therefore, we are never alone. Being single does not mean that you are unattractive or that no one wants you. *Psalms 13:14* says...."you were fearfully and wonderfully made". Being single simply means that God wants you to himself for a season before He places your spouse in your life.

Many of us, as single women, do not feel complete unless we are married or involved in a relationship with the opposite sex. The day that we became a new, converted Christian we begun the process of being made whole; our old nature passed away and behold all things became new in Christ Jesus. Although our desires changed, we must understand that there is also a process of purification and sanctification that we must go through. We read in the book of Esther that each woman had to prepare herself by going through purification for twelve long months, just for one night with the King. Sisters, the Lord wants to make you whole before He presents you to your king that He has ordained just for you. Tell me, who in their right mind, wants an incomplete man? No one in their right mind wants an incomplete man. Although, many of us may have experienced one in our lifetime and can testify that it was a rocky road headed to nowhere. So, if we as women are desiring men that are whole, then you better believe that men are looking for women that are whole. Our days of settling is over, especially when Daddy (our Heavenly Father) wants to give us the very best. I rather have a Boaz than a Bozo!

The bible says that in *Exodus 29:30* that as part of their purification, the priests daubed blood on their ears to be anointed to hear God's laws, and on their hands, so that they could do His will, and on their toes in order to be anointed to follow in His steps. My sisters, have you applied the blood to your ears - to hear our Father's instructions; to your hands - that you touch not the unclean thing and to your toes - that He may direct your paths? The Lord wants to purge you in order that He may bless you.

In order for us to function in a Godly manner in any relationship whether it is a marriage, friendship, fellowship with church members or co-workers or being a witness for Jesus, we must all possess a solid relationship with the Lord. We must be intimate with the Lord in prayer, worship and studying the Word of God. Without having a personal relationship with Jesus we will find out that eventually all other relationships will fail because He is the glue that holds relationships together. You find many people that have gone through a divorce before becoming a Christian often say, if I knew what I know now concerning the Word and the Power of Christ, I would have stayed in my marriage and allowed God to work it out.

People and relationships perish because of a lack knowledge. The enemy will always bring up something to destroy relationships because relationships are covenant and the devil does not like covenant!

Exodus 2:24-23
And God heard their groaning, and God remembered his covenant with Abraham, with Isaac, and with Jacob
And God looked upon the children of Israel, and God had respect unto them.

We must learn the importance of crying out to God and bringing back to His remembrance what He has promised us in His Holy Word. Many women more so than men, become very discouraged when they are not married by a certain age. I want to expose the spirit of deception that comes from the enemy that has blinded so many of our sisters and caused many to go into depression and give up on hope of ever having a blessed marriage. When it comes to God, age is just another number locked up in time and has no bearing on what God can or will do for an individual. We always want things when we want them and how we want them but sometimes God has a purpose and a plan for our lives past what our finite minds could even fathom. The bible says in the book of Genesis that Jacob served Laban for 14 years for Rachael. Jacob was willing to wait in order to receive what he really wanted and he refused to settle.

As a single woman, I learned so much about myself and the number one thing that I learned in my early stages was that I was not ready for marriage. I was ready for a fairytale and a sex life but not marriage. I needed to go through the process of being purged and delivered from my past relationships. I still had my former boyfriends on my mind and how they made me feel and I was comparing how I wanted my so-called Mr. Right to be with all of them. You see, I was single outwardly but not inwardly. I was still soul tied to my ex-lovers. I had not divorced them emotionally or mentally. Do you know that when you have intercourse with someone that you are performing an act of marriage. In biblical times a marriage was not made legitimate by standing before a preacher and signing a marriage license but a marriage was made legitimate by having sexual intercourse with that person. Sex is what consummated the marriage. Sisters, how many times have you been married and have you gotten a divorced?

I remember one night I felt an urgency to go into intercessory prayer. I was living a Godly life as a single woman keeping myself from defiling my temple (my body) with fornication but I was still bound to lustful dreams of my past sexual relationships. I did not feel single at all, I felt emotionally tied to my ex-lovers. I remember falling on my face crying out to God asking him to break every soul tie that I had encountered through sexual intercourse. I wanted the memories to be erased and the feelings to be gone; I needed to be made whole.

I did not want God to place the man that He had for me in my life and I was still thinking about my ex-lovers. I wanted to be free in my spirit and in my mind. I remember telling God, when you bless me with a husband, I want to be able to give him ALL of me and I don't want thoughts of anyone else in my mind but of him. I began to call out my ex-lovers names and commanded that their spirit come out of me. I remember the warfare I experienced when I called one person's name out, I had been emotionally (not physically) tied to him for years and as I cried out to God, I could feel Him literally breaking every soul tie and freeing my spirit and making me complete in Him. I remember when I got up from prayer, I felt light and a sense of wholeness overshadowed me. There were no more dreams and thoughts of men of my past, I was single FOR REAL! I was free to love the man God placed in my life as my husband with all of me.

Many of us love the ideal of being married but do you know what being married entails? I can talk from both sides because I know what it feels like and what it is to be a young single Christian woman, then married, and divorced. Marriage is sacrifice, giving of yourself to your spouse, changing some of your ways in order to please him and knowing what it takes and what it means to build a relationship that will last for a life time. Sisters, if your main desire for wanting to get married is because you cannot keep your flesh under subjection, than that is not a good enough of a reason. When you speak this, what you are really saying is that I don't believe God is able to keep me and I need a substitute for God! Allow God to make you whole so that His perfect will may be done in your life. Marriage is not the remedy to lust, deliverance is. Many people get married instead of dealing with the spirit of lust and find themselves committing adultery after they get married because they never dealt with the spirit of lust.

In *Mark 10:46-52*, we read of blind Bartimaeus sitting along the highway begging for alms and as he was sitting there, he heard a great multitude of people walking bye and he asked what was all the commotion about and they told him that Jesus of Nazareth was passing bye. When blind Bartimaeus heard that Jesus was passing bye, he began to cry out, "Jesus thou Son of David, have mercy on me!" The people tried to shut him up but he cried out even the louder, "Jesus thou Son of David, have mercy on me!" When Jesus heard his cry for help, the bible declares that JESUS STOOD STILL and COMMANDED that he be brought to Him. Jesus recognized the CRY that Bartimaeus had made. There was sincerity and a despairing cry for change heard in Bartimaeus' voice. Therefore, Jesus came to his rescue and caused him to receive his sight. When you really want to receive deliverance, God will come to your rescue. Jesus asked Bartimaeus, what will you have me to do and Bartimaeus said that I might receive my sight and Jesus answered and said "YOUR FAITH HAS MADE THEE WHOLE". If you want to be made whole, all you have to do is cry out to the Lord in sincerity and make your petitions known unto Him and He will not only answer you, but He will deliver you and make you whole!

Faith in Christ Jesus is what makes a person whole. A woman who has been made whole is a woman who has balance; she knows who she is and where she is going. She does not compromise or settle because she knows that she can have the very best that God has to offer. If you feel that you are incomplete because you are not married, or if you feel that you cannot make it without having a man in your life, then you have not been made whole. There is yet an inward healing that you need to receive. An *incomplete* person, is one who is double minded, whose emotions are imbalanced, who is not sure of herself, who always seeks other's approval or influence and one who cannot make a decision on her own. I have been there, it was like I was on a roller coaster ride with no clarity of what I wanted out of life and not sure of my own identity. I was in desperate need to be made whole. My first step was confronting my issues, to admit them and conqueror them. No one likes to admit that they have issues (problems) or have low self-esteem. We like to cover things up and pretend but God wants to uncover the scars and apply some sap (the word of God) to the wounds so that they may heal properly. Even though you are not married right now, you can save your future marriage by becoming a whole individual. Being whole will keep you from a lot of unnecessary arguments and you can use that same energy you would have used arguing on making love to your spouse or spending quality time with your family.

Your first step to being made whole is to deal with YOU and stop looking for fault in everyone else. Your greatest investment in life, should be made in yourself! Making sure that you are WHOLE, healed and content in whatever state in life you may be in. If you don't love you, then how do you expect anyone else to love you?

Are you ready to take the necessary Steps to becoming whole?

Philippians 4:13
I can do all things through Christ which strengtheneth me.

STEP 1— *Confession and Confrontation* were my first steps to wholeness. Sometimes looking in a mirror can be a scary sight when you have never dealt with the real you! I had to confess and then confront my failures and weaknesses. I had to make them known unto the Lord, who is faithful and just to not only forgive me but also heal me. (*James 5:16*) I had suffered rejection in my adolescent years; therefore, it was hard for me to trust and love whole heartily without thinking that someone had a plot to hurt me in the end. I had so much pain and disappointment on the inside of me that I had never dealt with but suppressed them over the years. I knew that I could not carry those yokes of bondage into a marriage. I had experienced broken relationship after broken relationship because I was looking for love in all the wrong places and never once did I stop to look in the mirror. We must be honest with ourselves and with God if we expect to receive His deliverance. A lack of honesty keeps us held bondage in certain areas of our lives. Your confession and confrontation is what brings forth your deliverance. Ask the Lord to show you yourself and bring to light anything that is in your heart that is not of Him. I promise you that He want leave you like He finds you. Don't be afraid to confront your issues. Open up yourself to the Lord and allow him to break every generational curse; heal you of your past and allow Him to minister His love to you. Don't allow what you went through in your past to hinder what God wants to do in your future. God wants to make love to you my sister. He makes love to you by shaping and molding you into His own image and then giving you an expected end.

Psalm 139:23-24
"Search me, O God and know my heart,
try me and know my thoughts
And see if there be any wicked way in me
and lead me in the way everlasting.

  Through the power of prayer and fasting, I received my healing and personal restoration that enabled me to trust and love whole heartily.

  STEP 2— *Forgiveness*, you must be willing to forgive those who have hurt you in your past. Forgiveness produces liberty. In order to be set free you must forgive, (*Matthew 6:14-15*). Many women have suffered from low self-esteem, sexual, verbal and even physical abuse. Many of these things were develop from the experience of abusive relationships, childhood dysfunction, broken marriages, etc. and because healing never manifested in them, they have grown up bitterness and unforgiveness locked up in their hearts. You can never be free to love completely or experience true love until you receive deliverance in those areas of your life and forgive those who have violated or hurt you. When you have suffered from these types of traumatic events, the effect of them, wounds your soulish man, which is the seat of your emotions. You will never be balanced in life until you get your emotions together. You may be saying like I once did, "how do I forgive, when it hurts so badly"? Have you ever been so broken that when you went down to pray no words would come out of your mouth? You could only utter moaning and groanings to the Lord. My sisters, I have been there, at a place where revenge seemed more logic than forgiving, when hate felt easier than forgiving. In *Romans 12:19* the Lord says that vengeance belongs to Him; that He would repay. When we try to fight our own battles or take revenge out on a person that has hurt us, we only make the situation worst and open the door for more spirits to enter into us. The word of God is like a hammer it breaks up our fallow ground which is the hard places in our lives and makes our hearts tender; ready to receive instruction from the Word of God. Our Heavenly Father has given us instruction to forgive those who have wronged us in any way, to love our enemies and to do good to them, (*Matthew 6:27-37*). Remember forgiveness produces liberty and liberty opens the door for your spiritual growth. Once a person is set free by the power of God they become teachable ready to be molded into a vessel of honor.

STEP 3—*Commitment,* Once you have confessed and confronted your issues and have forgiven those who have wronged you, you must commit yourself to the Lord in prayer, applying the word to your daily life and fasting that you may maintain your focus.

Proverbs 16:3
"Commit thy works unto the Lord, and thy thoughts shall be established"

Single women must create a healthy discipline in their lives and commit themselves to the work of the ministry and to the obedience of Christ. By committing ourselves to the Lord and His work we allow Him to shape us and develop our character. I have literally given myself over to the Lord in the work of the ministry and I find it to be my greatest joy. When I occupy myself with the work of the ministry, it leaves less time for idleness and it keeps me focus on the right things. Not only must we commit ourselves to the work of the ministry but we must also commit ourselves to being honest with ourselves and the way we feel on the inside. You are your best judge, because no one knows you better than yourself. The question is, do you have enough integrity to acknowledge your flaws when the Lord reveals them to you or when you see them? Christian singles often complain that there is not enough things to do in the church to keep them occupied or to keep their minds off of sex, but *1 Corinthians 7:34b* says……*the unmarried woman careth for the things of the Lord, that she may be holy both in body and in spirit.* There is so much to do in the Lord, but we tend to focus more on doing the things that satisfy the flesh. We must commit ourselves to things that have meaning that will enable us to grow not only spiritually but also financially. One way of occupying yourself is to commit yourself to your goals that you have allowed to lie dormant and have not brought into fruition. Take this time as a single woman and commit to building yourself up spiritually, financially and physically. Our time is of essence and must be spent wisely.

Commitment begins by making yourself available to something or someone (leadership, goals, education, etc.). When Boaz took notice of Ruth she was so committed to gleaning the harvest in order to take back provision to Naomi, that she did not even see him. He had to ask his servants, whose Damsel is this? (*Ruth 2:5*). Let your Boaz find you committed to the work of the ministry or pioneering in business and charitable works.

Chapter 2

IDENTITY CRISIS

Acts 19:15
....Jesus I know, and Paul I know, but who are ye?

In studying the creation in the Word of God, we learn our purpose for being here and why we were created. The Hebrew word for creation is *bara*, which is an activity that only God can do. It means that at a specific moment God called into existence matter and substance, which had no prior existence. The method God used in creation was the power of His Word. God said and it became! In *Genesis 1:26* God said let us the **Father,** who gave the command; **Jesus,** the administrator who is the powerful word through whom God created all things and the **Holy Spirit,** the *ruach*, breath and the wind of God who is pictured as moving over the creation preserving and preparing it for further creative activity. Everything that was created was created for a purpose. God created the Heavens and the Earth as a manifestation of His glory, majesty and power. The Heavens declare the glory of God and the firmament showeth His handiwork. The heavens and earth were created to receive back the glory and honor due Him. The Earth was also created in order to provide a place where His purpose and goals for humankind might be fulfilled.

Man and woman were both created in the image and likeness of God and on the basis of this image man could respond to and have fellowship with God and uniquely reflect His character. They were to do this by knowing God and obeying Him. They possessed a moral likeness to God, for they were created sinless and holy possessing wisdom, agape love, and the will to do the right thing. They lived in personal fellowship with God that involved moral obedience and personal communion. When Adam and Eve sinned, the moral likeness to God was corrupted and declined progressively in all men born after Adam and Eve and man took on a propensity to sin. Adam and Eve chose to become self-dependent instead of God-dependent. The whole human race plunged into chaos. Adam and Eve were created personal beings with spirit, mind, emotion, self-consciousness, and power of choice. Since the garden man has been in an identity crisis warring between two natures on the inside of them -- the flesh and the spirit. They have set their affections on earthly and materialistic things instead of heavenly things and have forgotten their true purpose. We lose sight of who we are when we step out of our covenant relationship with our Heavenly Father. We begin to act on our own will instead of God's will and we become more and more like the world and sin begins to cover the image of Christ in us until we return back to God in covenant relationship.

Through the storms of life many women have lost their sight of who they are and what their purpose is in life. *Proverbs 29:18* says, *"Where there is no vision, the people perish, but he that keepeth the law, happy is he".* The Hebrew word for vision is *hazon*, which means revelation. When we lose revelation of who we are, everything else in our lives begins to die such as our dreams, appearance and our joy. The Lord wants to restore to you your vision and personal identity so that you may walk in total victory. Many women have lost their true identity and sense of knowing who they are because they have tried to mimic others for so long. We have mirrored doing things like we see other people do them instead of asking God how He wants us to do it. We don't walk in our own identity but we try to look and dress like celebrities; we try to be like our parents; and/or we try to please people to get their acceptance until the crisis becomes alive in us. We lose sight of our own talents, abilities and creativity that god has given to us. It's time to strip off the masks and unveil the real you because God wants you to be the original masterpiece that he created as His original design. You are at your very best when you are simply being yourself. Stop trying to be like everyone else and just be you!

Your inner beauty lies in your true identity. No matter what shape, color or background you may come from, it has nothing to do with who God ordained you to be. The worst feeling one can have is to be unsure of who they are. Ester was an orphan who was a Jew in a pagan Palace as a runner up to be Queen. It would have seen as if she had everything working against her but when she decided to be herself and not dress or look like the other women, she was chosen above all other women in that providence to be Queen.

After becoming queen, Esther found herself in the midst of a crisis because she was still hiding her true identity of who she really was, a Jew. This not only jeopardized her life but the entire Jewish Nation. It was not until Esther revealed her true identity to the King that deliverance came to the entire Nation of Jews who had been scheduled to be executed by Haman.

In our personal relationship with the Lord we find out who we really are and what

He has destined us to be. It was when Esther sought the Lord in a 3 day fast that she was led to reveal her identity to the King. At any cost, she was ready to reveal her identity, she said "if I perish, I perish, but I am going to see the King". Women it's time to go see the King and allow Him to reveal our true identity to you. If you don't know who you are, it will be detrimental entering into a marriage, expecting that man to tell you or show you who you are.

As a single woman, you need time to find out your true identity before entering into a relationship. Many of us do not know who we really are or where we are going in life. The Lord wants you to discover the REAL YOU! He wants to create stability and accountability within you so you want settle for just anyone that comes your way and says "you are my wife". We tend to settle when we don't know our worth or true identity.

Have you ever been in a relationship and have been told "you need me because you can't make it without me" or "since you have a child outside of marriage, no one will want you". This is the spirit of deception and it lures many women into captivity in their minds and opens the door to low self-esteem to enter in. Once you receive this deception you find yourself in a place of brokenness and vulnerability. Many women have stayed in abusive relationships for a long period of time, because they did not know their worth. God has a plan and purpose for your life while you are single but first he wants you to discover your identity. Sisters, when you know who you are, no one can keep you in bondage.

Before I was born again I use to seek to date men with one thing in mind, can he pay my bills. I didn't look for the other important qualities like his personality, was he faithful and committed to a relationship, did he make his money legally but all my carnal mind thought about at the time, was show me the money! You see, I thought I needed a man in my life in order to make it and to take care of me but when I came into the knowledge of the truth (the Word of God) I realized that Jesus was my source and my Jehovah Jireh (my provider).

It was after my deliverance that the Lord began to reveal the talents, skills and abilities He had created on the inside of me to be a successful woman in life. I realized that I could make my own money and pay my own bills and buy my own materialistic things. This is when the qualities that I looked for in a man changed. I began to desire a man that was able to take me to my next spiritual level in God. I now desired someone who knew how to take care of responsibilities, one that feared God and loved the Lord with his whole heart. If he love God, then I knew he would know how to love me. Women don't sell out to things but sell out to God who can supply all your needs according to his riches in glory, (*Philippians 4:19*).

God wants you to start loving yourself and seeking Him for the plan He has ordained for your life before the foundation of the world. I remember when I was in high school; I use to dream the same dream over and over again. I dreamed that I was standing behind a podium before thousands of people delivering a speech and leading the people in a positive direction. Because I had no spiritual guidance in my life at that time nor was I saved at that time, I thought that once I became an adult that I would become the next woman Mayor for the City of Tampa. So I joined Student Government and every club there was in high school that had something to do with politics, trying to find my identity. Not knowing that years and years later that I would be called into ministry as a Senior Pastor leading thousands of souls to Christ through preaching the Word of God. I had always felt a strong sense of purpose for my life but I searched for my purpose in everything but God. I looked for it in men, careers and in the world but it was when I surrendered to the Lord that I found it in Christ Jesus.

In 1989 when I received Jesus Christ as my personal savior, He began to show me dreams and give me scriptures concerning my life, and then sent spirit led people to speak into my life concerning my destiny and what God had called me to do. They only confirmed what the Lord had already spoken and revealed to me. As I grew spiritually, I begin to allow the Lord to take off all the masks that I was wearing through the years trying to please everyone but Him. I stopped living for people and no longer did things to please others but I began living for my maker and my creator. He was the one who had forgiven me for all of my sins and who gave me a right to the tree of life and to Him belongs all the honor and glory.

I wanted to please Him with all my heart. I searched for my purpose in the scriptures and He told me in *Hebrews 12:2* that He was the author and finisher of my faith and in *Jeremiah 29:11* that He had given me an expected end. This gave me hope and faith to believe in myself again to let me know that there were hidden treasures in me that He wanted to unfold and reveal to the nation.

I needed to love me first in order for others to love me and before I could be free to love someone else. Sisters, a man cannot make you happy, if you are not first happy with yourself. We put too much responsibility on the man, we expect them to come into our lives and put all the broken pieces of our lives together when in essence Jesus is the only one who can do that. What makes YOU happy? Have you ever sat down and thought about that? When is the last time you thought about pleasing yourself?

I know that these questions are hitting home because we as women try to make everyone else happy but ourselves. As a single woman you need to enjoy who you are and soar! Enjoy your life; stop waiting for a man to come in the picture to enjoy life. Take yourself on a vacation, buy yourself some roses and celebrate the woman of God that you are! As a single woman, I took pleasure in my femininity and doing things that brought serenity to me. I love quiet time, so there were many times when I wanted to be pampered and relaxed, so I would put on a worship CD, draw a warm bubble bath, light my candles, get a good book and relax in the Lord. I try to enjoy life to the fullest and do things that make me happy. Through my many struggles of trying to please everyone else, it taught me many valuable lessons in life. Life is what you make it to be and your success and happiness is determined by the very choices that you make.

I remember when I was interested in this certain minister and to me he was everything that a Christian woman could ever desire in a mate. This young man had so many high expectations of how he wanted his wife to be such as what type of college degree he wanted her to have, how he wanted her to dress, act, preach, etc. I tried to fit all those roles to no avail; no matter what I did it was never good enough for him. He always made me feel like I was not good enough and always seemed to put me on a level lower than others. I remember whenever I had to preach or do something in front of him publicly I would always feel so intimidated or inadequate. I had to realize that he was just a mere man who did not deserve having me if he could not recognize my inner beauty and love me for who I was and for who God had created me to be.
    We do not have to succumb to the opinions of others! However, through this ordeal it made me stronger and more aware of the integrity and grace that the Lord had imparted in me. See my sisters, love gives; it does not take from you.

Chapter 3

THE MAKE-UP OF A WOMAN

1 Peter 3:3-4
3 Whose adorning let it not be that outward adorning of plaiting the hair, and of wearing of gold, or of putting on of apparel;

4 But let it be the hidden man of the heart, in that which is not corruptible, even the ornament of a meek and quiet spirit, which is in the sight of God of great price.

When we speak of the makeup of a woman, we think of it in the natural and think of cosmetic products that women use to beautify themselves. The bible says as it is in the natural so it is in the spirit. Make up is designed and used to beautify the complexion, eyes and lips to make women look younger and more attractive. It is the preparation to enhance beauty, improve the look of your skin and appearance. It is also used to cover up wrinkles and blemishes; however, it cannot cover up sin or the real you. When makeup is applied it changes the look of a woman, it makes her feel more confident about her appearance, it beautifies the outside but it does nothing for the inside. The inside is still broken, bruised and battered. Too long have we dealt with the outside and left the inside undone.

Women, we must learn our true identity, who we really are. It's not our makeup, our shape, our beauty or our careers but it's the Spirit of God that dwells on the inside of us that teaches, leads, guides and shapes us into vessels of honor.

When God created woman (Eve), He created her to be a helpmeet to Adam. This was done on the sixth day and was the grand climax of all that God had created during the creation week. Everything He created during the creation week from day one up until day six, He spoke into existence but on the sixth day when He made man, the bible says that He made man from the dust of the earth and breathed His own breath (*neshemah*) into man and man became a living soul. When it came to the woman the bible says that God put the man asleep (he did not need any interference), therefore God caused a sleep to fall upon Adam. The bible says that when God put Adam to sleep, THEN He pulled the rib out of Adam and created the woman from his rib. God caused it to be a deep sleep, so that the opening of Adam's side would not cause him any pain. See my sisters, God never intended for a woman to bring her man pain but when we don't know who we are we bring pain into the lives of those who we love.

We are like a roller coaster ride, up one minute and down the next. We must note that God took the woman from Adam's rib and not from his head to rule over him, or from his feet to be trampled upon by him but from his side to be equal with him. Under his arm to be protected by him and near to this heart to be loved by him.

We all were created in the image of God (*Genesis 1:27*); an image is a representation or replica of one person or thing by another and likeness means comparison. Therefore, we are to reflect His holiness at all times. *Proverbs: 31:29* says "*Many daughters have done virtuously but thou excellest them all*". We excel when we walk in His holiness and in His confidence that we are who He says that we are!

THERE ARE THREE THINGS THAT EVERY WOMAN SHOULD KNOW ABOUT HERSELF:

(1) **That you were created in God's image** and everything that you do must reflect His holiness. "What Would Jesus Do" must be a question that we ask ourselves before we act upon any situation. Knowing that you were created in God's image and after His likeness should boost your self-esteem.

(2) **You were created to give birth.** God told us to be fruitful and multiply and replenish the earth and to subdue it. Because of this, the enemy, from the beginning, has tried to abort, stop and kill our seed to no avail. The enemy comes to kill and destroy, not only our natural babies but also to our spiritual babies which are your dreams, ministry, gifts/talents, etc. Women you are creative and anointed to bring forth! There are so many treasures locked up on the inside of you!

(3) **God gave you dominion from the beginning**, which is authority and leadership ability. We were created to be leaders, therefore, walk in your

authority and do not allow the enemy to triumph over you. We must exercise our authority in the earth and live a victorious life!

Our spiritual makeup should consist of:

(1) Salvation
(2) A Godly Image
(3) Godly Character
(4) Integrity
(5) Motherhood
(6) Strength
(7) Honor
(8) Dignity
(9) Holiness
(10) Grace
(12) Sanctification
(13) Purpose
(14) Justification
(15) Forgiveness
(16) Faith
(17) Love
(18) Femininity
(19) Success
(20) Favor
(21) Inner Chastity
(22) Wholeness
(23) Anointing
(24) Accountability
(25) Faithfulness
(26) Leadership Ability

Chapter 4

DESIRING BUT NOT DESPERATE

Psalms 37:4-5
Delight thyself also in the lord; and he shall give thee the desires of thine heart
Commit thy way unto the Lord; trust also in him; and he shall bring it to pass.

Many times in the church single women and single men have been labeled as been lustful or anxious when they have made known that they are desiring companionship. Many Christian singles are afraid to make known that they have a desire to be married. I am here to tell you my sisters that there is absolutely nothing wrong with you desiring companionship and desiring to be married. We were created with a longing in us, to be connected to the man that God brought us out of. Don't feel ashamed or embarrassed to admit to the fact that you desire a husband. As a matter of fact, the bible tells us to make our petitions known unto the Lord who is faithful and just to bring them to pass. God has an assignment for every individual. Not everyone desires to be married but there are many that do and whatever our situation, to be married or to remain single, the main thing is to be able to express yourself freely to the

Lord and to be content in whatever state you are in. The bible says that Michal, Saul's daughter, loved David and she made it known unto her father and the thing pleased her father Saul and he gave her to David to be his wife. Women tell your Heavenly Father what you want and learn how to be specific in your prayer request because what you ask for is what you are going to get.

If you desire a Boaz or a King David then give God the resume and let Him search and seek him out and bring him to you in due season. The power of release is in knowing how to present your petition to the Lord and your petition must line up with the Word of God. *Habakkuk 2:2* says to write the vision and make it plain. Therefore, if you desire to be married, you should write down a list of the qualities that you seek in a companion and pray the vision. Now, the word of the Lord says to make it plain, meaning be specific in your request. If you want him mature, handsome, SAVED, financially stable, family oriented and physically fit then write it down on your personal prayer list and take it before the Lord in prayer with the expectation that you will receive just what you asked for. As a single woman of integrity and Godly character, you must have a standard of what type of mate you are seeking and not allow anything or anyone to detour you from that standard that you have set. Many women lower their standards when they become frustrated and impatient with waiting, so they compromise and settle. Settling is a mistake that can often lead to spiritual death, divorce, bitterness, adultery, etc. We must understand the danger of allowing our desires to turn into desperation.

When you look up the word *desire* in the Webster Dictionary it means to wish or long for, want, to ask for, solicit or request. A desire is to wish strongly for something that is or seems to be within reach. To me, a desire is an emotion or longing created by God and we must allow Him, through the Holy Spirit to govern the type of desires that we have. We must understand that there is a difference between "need and "desire". There are many things that we think we need but a true need is something that is a necessity or to have a true deficiency of something essential in life or something needed to fulfill God's purpose in life. A desire, on the other hand, is not something that is essential, but something which is enjoyable in the process of fulfilling God's purposes.

THREE AREAS OF NEED AND DESIRE:

(1) The ***physical part*** of us, is through our bodies. This unique part of us longs to be touched, embraced, stimulated and to feel loved. It desires to be intimate, to be comfortable and pampered. When these needs and desires are not met, we experience a physical discomfort and if not careful we begin to defile the body with the works of the flesh such as fornication and adultery. (Galatians 5:19-21). We must learn how to fill this desire through worship and becoming intimate with our savior and also by learning how to love ourselves. So many people confuse making love with having sex, there is a difference. When you make love you stimulate not only your physical desires but also the mind and emotions when you experience it with your mate.

(2) The ***psychological part*** of us includes our mind, intellect, will and emotions. It longs to feel loved, secure, and protected; it also longs for companionship, healthy relationships and intimacy with others. This unique part of us desires wholeness, stability and trust. It longs for companionship where you can share your thoughts, ideas and dreams with someone and it longs for someone to understand you. When these desires and needs are not satisfied, we are no longer balanced; we feel a loss of trust and open up the door for low self-esteem and brokenness. Therefore, we must choose mates that know how to communicate and express love. To be equally yoked means more than just the two of you being saved, but do you have common goals, can he communicate on your level, does he have a vision for his life and can move you into your next level with God. To be in a relationship with someone that you cannot have a mature conversation with becomes frustrating, you become alone and lose interest in them because you feel lonely and void of communication and we, as women, love to communicate!

(3) The ***spiritual part*** of us, which needs to be nurtured with the things of God and desires constantly to be filled with the spirit, wisdom, knowledge and righteousness of God. If we are not joined to someone who is spiritual; who can usher us into the presence of God; and who can minister to us when we are broken, as time goes by, we will become irritated with them. When we experience a deficiency in this area of our lives, it leads to spiritual death and destruction. One of the most miserable feelings, as a saved woman, is to be married to someone void of a spiritual life, who does not understand the things of God and who cannot minister to you spiritually. In this day and time, many women have walked in the role of leadership in every aspect of life to the point that they are saying "when the men are going to take their rightful place?" The man's position in his home is to be the "Priest" of his home and as we read in the bible the priest position in the temple was to make sure that everything was in order in the house of God and that the people were in right standing with God. So it is in the natural so it is in the spirit. As the man being the priest of his home, his role in the home is to first lead his family to Christ and make sure that his household is living out the word of God in their lives and to be that provider and protector of his home.

The Word of God says that, if we delight ourselves in the Lord, that He would give us the desires of our heart. Simply put, our desire must be in the perimeter of God's word in order for His will to be fulfilled in our lives. If you are saved then you must pray for a saved companion. Our desires and motives must be put in perspective because God cannot and will not go against His own will. We read throughout the Old Testament how God instructed the Children of Israel not to marry anyone from a heathen nation who did not serve the true and living God. If you are a born again believer and you join yourself to someone who is an unbeliever, you step out of the perfect will of God and open yourself up for failure in your relationship and even in your spiritual life.

Women, desire a man of God, choose what God has ordained and not after the manner of your own flesh. Women that are attractive to the "bad boys" or "thugs" as we say, (*which were the types of men that use to be my forte before I was delivered, thank God for deliverance*), are often women who have some type of void in their lives and seek for fulfillment and love through sex, power and excitement. Bad Boys have a strong sex appeal and many women find them irresistible and intriguing but are miserable when they hook up with them because he can only please their flesh and cannot commit to a meaningful relationship because a "bad boy" my sisters cannot be trusted, he is a ladies man and thrives off of his male ego which tells him to try and seduce and have as many women as he can while dealing with you at the same time. He is all about game and his flesh cannot be tamed without the power of God working within him.

These types of men are not emotionally but are physically driven. Many women allow good men to pass them by because they are tied to a fantasy -- thinking that they can change the "bad boy" they have become emotionally tied to. Many women think that they have what it takes to make him change but the truth is; only God can change him and you will spend effortless time trying to make him something that he does not desire to be! Let's be real chances are, if he does not change before you marry him, he won't change after you marry him. So don't be deceived, the chance is too risky to take, your future, your peace, joy and destiny depends on it.

Many women fall into this deception because they feel that there are no available men in the church and they start looking outside the covenant. If God can take five fishes and two loaves of bread and feed 5,000 people, surely he can supply you a Boaz. Rumor has it that there is a man shortage and not enough men in the church so the women of God start settling for a half of a man or an unsaved man who does not even believe in your God. This my sisters is a spirit of deception and lack of faith in the church. I know that when we look around the church that there are more women than there are men but I truly believe that God has someone for all of us and that we do not have to step out of the covenant to get him, God does not work like that.

THE DANGER OF BEING DESPERATE

Judges 14:3
Then his father and his mother said unto him, is there never a woman among the daughters of thy brethren, or among all my people, that thou goest to take a wife of the uncircumcised Philistines? And Samson said unto his father, Get her for me for she pleases me well.

Although, the Lord had blessed Samson tremendously and placed a heavy anointing upon him from his birth, Samson's desires for certain type of women were not pleasing not only to his parents but they were also not pleasing to God. We must long for and ask for Godly companions. Samson made ungodly decisions that eventually led him to spiritual failure and physical death because he choose a wife from his fleshly desires. He was motivated by his own desires which were to seek marriage outside of God's will. James 1:14 tell us that every man is tempted when he is drawn by his own lust and enticed. In other words, temptation is birthed from our own inward desires. If the Spirit of God does not purge our ungodly desires, then they lead to sin and cause us to make choices outside of the will of God.

I don't care how long you may have been saved and how strong or anointed you may think you are, you cannot change an individual -- that is a job for Jesus alone. I went into a marriage knowing that my husband was not my equal and not up to the part in his Christian walk. You see, I allowed my flesh to get in the way of my choosing. I allowed his good looks, the attention that he showed me and the notion that I could change him and help mold him into what God wanted him to be blindfolded me. My thinking that I was anointed enough for both of us and that I could change him was foolish thinking. What a mistake I made, not knowing how much it would cost me just by saying "I Do" at the wrong time and to the wrong man. It almost caused me a nervous breakdown! I suffered hurt, humiliation, infidelity, and a painful divorce. I also experienced a great setback in my ministry.

It took years for me to get back in my rightful place with the Lord. I had allowed myself to become frustrated with prior relationships that had failed and did not work out and I became weary in my waiting and made a choice to settle instead of trusting in God. Maybe if I had waited on God to finish his complete work in my ex-husband before we got married, we would not have ended up in divorce court. He was a good man with great potential but had not been purged and seasoned in the Lord. I grabbed him from off of the potter's wheel when God was still trying to mold and make him. Many women make this mistake in the church. You have been saved for a while and seasoned in the Lord and soon as a brother joins the church and get saved, we are like vultures grabbing for what God has not even offered to us.

The bible says that He (not she) that findeth a wife finds a good thing for his life. When we start choosing we seek after the manner of our flesh. We break the brother's focus off of God and where God is trying to take him and places his focus on us and enter into a relationship prematurely. He never develops into the man of God that God intended for him to be because we allowed our flesh to interrupt the master plan of God for his life. We enter in the relationship excited and feeling good but after a month or two when the excitement of pleasing the flesh by way of sex has died down and our spirit man needs to be strengthened and ministered to, that man has nothing to offer us because we pulled him off the potter's wheel too soon. We become frustrated and irritated by everything that he does because he is not able to satisfy our intellect or lead us spiritually.

Perhaps you are in this place right now, you are in a relationship with someone or considering marrying someone and the warnings signs are starring you right in the face and they are saying: "STOP, DO NOT ENTER, DEAD END, CAUTION OR CONSTRUCTION AHEAD:. Take heed to the warning signs my sisters and don't let desperation take you down the wrong road for once you have traveled a great distance down that road you end up having to make a U-turn in the middle of the marriage. The warning signs may be: he's not saved, he's an undercover homosexual, he's not responsible, he's not mature, he's not spiritually mature yet, he's not ready for commitment, or he's not financially stable. Whatever they may be take heed to them and wait on the Lord.

LET'S TALK ABOUT WARNING SIGNS AND THEIR PURPOSE.

The **"For Rent Sign"** means that you can enter in the relationship but it's going to cost you something and are you willing to pay the price? When you rent something you pay for it as you go and when the lease is up you have to move out unless you renew the lease. Many men have the for rent sign up, they only want you for what you can give them for the time being, they refuse to commit to marriage. These are the type of men that want sex and nothing else. You will even find them hiding in the church. You have to cut them off and not give them the time of day or you will fall into a dangerous sex trap mixed with emotional confusion.

"The Yield Sign" means slow down, you are going too fast. The Lord wants you to take your time, don't rush it but allow God to do his perfect work. Perhaps there are some things that God needs to do in you and in him before he puts the two of you together as husband and wife. Philippians 4:6 "Be careful (anxious) for nothing; but in everything by prayer and supplication with thanksgiving let your requests be made known unto God". Remember what God has for you, it is for you. Become friends before you become anything else this will cause the relationship to be much stronger and the communication line to open.

"The Do Not Enter Sign" is usually put up when God is trying to tell you, he's not good for you and will not be good to you. If you go this way, there is going to be danger ahead and it could cost you your salvation or even your life. This sign is also put up when the opposite sex, is an undercover homosexual, a counterfeit or already married. I know he looks good baby girl but never judge a book by its cover but by what's on the inside. You may ask "homosexuals and counterfeits in the church?" Yes, this spirit is rampant everywhere. Pray and ask God for the gift of discernment when seeking a companion and allow the Holy Spirit to speak and minister to you, because He will reveal to you if this is the one for you but you have to be in a spiritual place to receive truth and you must be spiritually sensitive to His voice. If he is already married, you already know DO NOT ENTER, WRONG WAY! Never settle being a side chic, mistress or someone's sex toy. Fornication is sin and all adulterers; the bible says, God will judge!

"The No U Turn Sign" is saying God has given you warning after warning but you refused to let the relationship go. The Lord has spoken to you and has said this is not what I have for you and if you do it (get married to that person) there is going to be no turning back. You find many married couples that have made a vow before God when they said "I Do" and have realized that it was the wrong time or perhaps with the wrong person and they are stuck in a relationship that only makes them miserable. Perhaps this is your last warning before you say "I Do" to the wrong person and the No U Turn Sign is ever before your face. Sister, DON'T DO IT, DON'T DO IT, DON'T DO IT!! Listen to the voice of God and allow the Holy Spirit to govern your decision making. Marrying the wrong man is not worth it in the long run; I don't care how good he looks or how anointed he may be, did God tell you to marry him or not?

"The Stop Sign" means to discontinue or cause to cease, to prevent from moving forward. There are relationships in our lives that we need to cut off and we must discontinue before our feelings become more involved and it becomes more difficult to cut off. If you find yourself in a relationship where you have been playing house and doing what only married folks are legal to do, it's time to STOP! Or perhaps the other person takes more from you than what they give to you or if they are pressuring you to compromise your standard, then you need to cut the relationship off. In many instances the stop sign is saying enough is enough how long will you abide in sin?

"Under Construction Sign" simply means God is still working on him, so leave him alone until God is finish making him, building him, molding him, healing him and prospering him. Nothing is more frustrating than getting with someone who is not spiritually, emotionally, or financially able to minister to your needs. *Lamentations 3:25 The LORD is good unto them that wait for him, to the soul that seeketh him.* What God has for you, is for you. Be patience and allow God to do his perfect work in an individual. Once he comes off the Potter's Wheel, he will be all that you desired him to be.

You must control your desire when it comes to desiring a mate so that it does not turn into desperation. When you allow yourself to become desperate your discernment is not keen and you tend to settle for the counterfeit and miss the real man that God has ordained for your life. This happens when you become anxious and fail to wait and seek God for direction in choosing your mate. Women you do have a choice! You have many men that come to churches seeking out weak women and women that they know they can prey on; the bible calls them "silly women".

When you look up the word counterfeit in the dictionary it means: imitation with intent to deceive, not genuine but forged. In other words he knows that he is not what he appears to be, he will camouflage himself as a man of God or something that he is not to gain your trust and attention to draw you into his nest only to give you a rude awakening after you have made the mistake of saying "I Do".

My sisters, it's okay to desire marriage but don't allow the enemy to make you desperate.

Chapter 5

PUTTING FLESH UNDER SUBJECTION

Galatians 5:16
This I say then, walk in the Spirit and ye shall not fulfill the lust of the flesh.

Many Christian singles have had a problem with keeping their flesh under subjection and yielding to the temptations of the flesh. This has been a struggle for many in the Body of Christ for decades. The battle is within the Christian himself and the conflict will continue until true deliverance is brought forth in that individual. It does not stop when you get married. Many think or feel that the antidote to putting the flesh under subjection is by getting married. Yes, the bible does say that it is better to marry than to burn but the antidote to crucifying the flesh is the Word of God and the power of the Holy Ghost working in your life.

The truth of the matter is that after you are married the devil will still tempt you with sex outside the marriage covenant. A single person must not look at wanting to get married just to have sex. Marriage goes far beyond two people being satisfied through sexual intercourse; marriage is a covenant between two people who love one another and want to share the rest of their lives together in the sight of the Lord.

Marriage entails *building*, *bonding* and *bearing*.

(1) Building a lifelong relationship with one another in spite of each other's weaknesses,
(2) Bonding together in love, unity and in the spirit of the Lord that God might be glorified through the marriage covenant, and by
(3) Bearing (fruit) children unto the Lord who will grow up and call you blessed.

I can remember when I first received salvation; I was so in love with the Lord and I longed to be in his presence at all times. I remember looking at the clock at work wanting 5:00 p.m. to hurry up and come so I could go home and fall on my face before the Lord in prayer and worship. I instantly became a lover of God's word and a seeker of His face but I still had an issue, MY FLESH. In receiving Christ as my personal savior I gave up just about everything, clubbing and drinking which I was never good at because alcohol never did agree with my body. I would take two sips of my alcoholic beverage and would instantly become intoxicated. I gave up the cursing, lying, etc. but I had a struggle when it came to giving up sex. During that time in my life I was dating an unsaved man who was use to the ways of the world and who did not understand God laws concerning premarital sex. I was hooked on the wrong lover, someone who knew how to please my flesh but could do nothing for my spirit. You see, I was looking for love but I was looking for it in all the wrong places. After the moments of pleasure were over, guilt would rush over me, tears would fall down my cheeks and my heart would cry out for forgiveness and then I would turn to my lover and tell him what a mistake it was and that this was not the will of God but a few months later, I would find myself right back in a defiled bed again doing the same old routine, enjoying the moments of pleasure because during the time of pleasure, your mind is consumed with how good it feels and not how displeasing it is to God. The flesh is a mess and craves to be pleased but if you want deliverance you have to starve the flesh of the very thing that it craves for and being a single person, nine times out of ten its SEX.

MY DELIVERANCE

Many people have wondered, do saved single people really and truly abstain from sex? The answer is yes, it can and is being done. I lived a life of celibacy for 16 years before marriage and found that it was not a struggle but my reasonable service to present my body to God as a living sacrifice, holy and acceptable unto Him. I completely sold out to God and placed Him first in my life above everything else including satisfying my flesh. I decreased that He could increase in my life with power, wisdom, knowledge, prosperity, etc. My body is the temple of the Holy Ghost, in other words it's the place where God dwells. He has chosen my body to house His spirit and the bible plainly states that He will not dwell in any unclean place.

Your body becomes unclean when you lay it down in an undefiled bed (premarital sex) and as you continue in sin the spirit of God moves out and many unclean spirits enter in. You open yourself up to all types of perversion.

Many single women and men, have asked me "how do you keep your flesh under subjection?" My answer to them is learning how to be intimate with God as it fulfils my every purpose and brings balance to my life. I had to learn that having a man did not make me complete but having Jesus did. You see, when I had a man in my life, I was still incomplete, broken and lonely. I learned, through the process of my deliverance, that I control this body (my flesh) and this body (my flesh) does not control me. Of course, in the beginning of my salvation, I thought that not being sexually involved with the opposite sex as a single woman, could not be done; but what I was doing was under estimating the power of God in my life.

I looked at my mother, a very strong woman of God who remained celibate for over 25 years of her life and who walked in integrity and refused to compromise. I drew strength from her and her lifestyle of holiness. She was my role model as a Christian Single woman walking out the word of God in her everyday life that exemplified holiness. My mom raised 5 beautiful girls as a single parent raised us to be virtuous women. I know that it was the power of God that kept my mother all those years because if you knew her testimony (next book) you will understand the depths of my words. I drew strength and motivation from her and I believe that every single woman and every single man need a strong role model in their lives, one who is *walking out* the word and from whom they can glean wisdom.

Many fail and yield to the temptations of the flesh because of association. Why associate yourself with someone who has the same weaknesses as you do? Can the blind lead the blind, NO! You may have failed in the past or you may have failed recently, guess what a brand new day has dawned, so pick up your defiled bed and cast it out and make your confession right now that you will no longer lay your body down in sin because your anointing is too valuable to spill or loose.

The bible says if you resist the devil, he will flee from you. That word *resist* means to oppose or to protect, you must oppose the desires, temptations and lust of the flesh and protect your body from becoming defiled. You must make up in your mind that you will give your body over to God to use as an honorable vessel to proclaim his work here on the earth and that you will not lay this body down in any sexual acts until you say I do. This has been my vow and I stand on it yet today. I stand as a prophetic voice and warn you against sexual sin as it wastes sexuality on unsatisfying and unloving relationships when sex ought to be preserved for the long-lasting, productive joy of marriage. I tried it the wrong way so many times, (sex before marriage) and found myself left alone with soul ties that lingered on the inside of me for years. In my time of being single and saved, I learned my worth and that sex before marriage was no longer an option or compromise, it is obsolete. I choose to remain pure before God.

I have a few questions to ask you and I want you to be honest with yourself:

1. Have you had premarital sex since you have been born again?

2. Do you still battle with sexual thoughts and dreams?

3. Do you masturbate to satisfy your sexual appetite?

4. Do you have a problem with your eyes, always looking and lusting after someone in the wrong manner?

5. Is getting married always on your mind?

6. Do you constantly battle with feeling lonely?

7. Do you stake claim to every single man that comes in the church to be your husband?

Galatians 5:16 say that if you walk in the spirit, you will not fulfill the lust of the flesh. If your answer is yes to two or more of the above questions, its ok, we have all been there and done that. It's just time for you to walk in your total deliverance. To walk in a victorious realm over the will of your flesh, you must learn how to abide in covenant relationship with the Lord. As long as we remain on this earth, there will be a constant battle within every believer whether he or she will surrender to the inclinations of the flesh or continue to yield to Holy Spirit. Jesus said in **John 15:4** Abide in me, and I in you. As the branch cannot bear fruit of itself, except it abide in the vine; no more can ye, except ye abide in me. Only when we abide in Christ, do we bear the fruit of the spirit. However, when we step outside of the Spirit and become weak by not yielding to the voice, word and the leading of the Holy Spirit, we allow the flesh to rule and this is when the works of the flesh begin to manifest in our lives which are these according to **Galatians 5:19-21**:

1. **<u>Adultery</u>** – Sexual relations of a married person with someone other than his or her spouse.
2. **<u>Fornication</u>** – Immoral sexual conduct and intercourse; it includes taking pleasure in pornographic pictures, films, or writing.
3. **<u>Uncleannes</u>** – Sexual sins, evil deeds and vices, including thoughts and desires of the heart.

4. **Lasciviousness** - Sensuality, following one's passions and desires to the point of having no shame or public decency.
5. **Idolatry** - Worship of spirits, persons, or graven images, also trust in any person, institution, or thing as having equal or greater authority than God and His word.
6. **Witchcraft** - Sorcery, spiritism, black magic, worship of demons, and use of drugs to produce spiritual experiences.
7. **Hatred** - Intense, hostile intentions and acts, extreme dislike or enmity.
8. **Variance** - Quarreling, antagonism, a struggle for superiority.
9. **Emulations** - Resentfulness, envy of another's success.
10. **Wrath** - Explosive anger or rage with flares into violent words and deeds.
11. **Strife** - Selfish ambition and seeking of power.
12. **Seditions** - Introducing divisive teachings not supported by the Word of God.
13. **Heresies** - Division within the congregation into selfish groups or cliques, with destroy the unity of the church.

14. **Envyings** - Resentful dislike of another person who has something that one desires.
15. **Murders** - Killing a person unlawfully and with malice.
16. **Drunkenness** - Impairing one's mental or physical control by alcoholic drink.
17. **Revellings** - Excessive feasting, revelry, a party spirit involving alcohol, drugs, sex or the like.

Let's look at the definition of the word *flesh*. The *flesh* Hebrew - Basar) and (Greek - Sarx) is the physical part of the body of humans which is called our sinful nature and is governed only by the power of God. We become weak when we lose fellowship with God. In other words when we don't show up to church, to prayer or to bible study, we allow our spirit to become weak and then Satan begins to send thoughts to the mind to weaken the spirit even greater. Sin is an act in the mind before it is ever acted out in the natural that is why we have to constantly cast down imaginations. It is so good to have "Girlfriend Relationships" to have sisters in the Lord that you can fellowship with outside the church who is strong in the Lord and seeking to please God in all their ways. We, as Christian women, need to learn how to enjoy life; we take being saved overboard at times.

We forget about living and enjoying life to the point that we become so self-righteous and secluded that we don't even know how to function properly outside the church. This is a religious spirit!

When is the last time you hung out with your girlfriends and laughed and cried over a good movie? These times are crucial in a single's woman's life. You need to find enjoyment and fellowship with others to occupy your time in a positive manner. Yes, you must stay busy doing the things of God but there is also life outside of the church and you must learn how to enjoy your life!

The key to putting your flesh under subjection is to renew the spirit of your mind. The mind can take you places the body has not yet gone but if you continue to think on those things, you will find yourself even as Paul did, doing the very things that you thought you would not do. Learn how to control and filter your thought life because what you think on the longest becomes the strongest in your life. It's ok to have sexual desires; God created us with these healthy desires but only for the marriage covenant. However, it becomes sin when you allow these thoughts to consume and overtake you and you find yourself acting out those desires.

WHAT IS SIN?

James 4:17 *Therefore to him that knoweth to do good, and doeth it not, to him it is sin.*

I John 3:4 *Whosoever committeth sin transgresseth also the law: for sin is the transgression of the law.*

Mark 7:20-23 *[20] And he said, That which cometh out of the man, that defileth the man. [21] For from within, out of the heart of men, proceed evil thoughts, adulteries, fornications, murders,*

[22] Thefts, covetousness, wickedness, deceit, lasciviousness, an evil eye, blasphemy, pride, foolishness:

[23] All these evil things come from within, and defile the man.

Chapter 6

The Dating Game

Philippians 4:6
Be careful for nothing; but in everything by prayer and supplication with thanksgiving let your requests be made known unto God.

Dating in Christendom can be a serious issue. We, as Christians have a standard and code of ethics that we must live by -- based upon the word of God. There are many different views on Christian dating, whether a Christian should date or not. I strongly believe that you should date someone at least 6 months to a year, if not longer, in order to get to know them before considering marriage. Many times in the church world, men and women have been single and celibate for quite a while and when they meet a potential mate, they rush the relationship before they really get to know one another and instead of falling in love, they fall in lust. They have an eagerness to have sex more than they have an eagerness to establish a friendship and then, perhaps a beautiful marriage. This is a dangerous place to be in that is why we must be strong in; the Lord and in the power of His might when it relates to becoming intimate with the opposite sex.

3 John 1:2 says: "Beloved, I wish above all things that thou mayest prosper and be in health, even as thy soul prospereth", meaning that God is concerned and desires for you to have the very best in every area of your life! This most definitely includes a relationship with the opposite sex.

Let's look at the word *intimate*, the Webster Dictionary defines it as affectionate, a familiar friend, acquaintance or to understand someone. Intimate does not always involve sensuous or sexual acts but it can simply mean to have a personal and platonic relationship with the opposite sex. *Philippians 4:6* tell us not to be anxious for anything, therefore we must take dating slow and learn about the person that we are establishing a relationship with. At times, women tend to be vulnerable and needy when it comes to a relationship with the male gender; we become blind to all the warning signs telling us that perhaps this may not be the one. Remember what we talked about in the first chapter, we must be **WHOLE** before entering into a relationship in order for us to be able to stand our ground during the dating process.

Remember dating is not to be indulged in when you are just simply trying to kill time or to get a free meal; but dating is for mature Christians only who are seeking marriage. When dating, you should date for friendship and selection of a mate, not just to kill time!

Before you consider dating someone, ask yourself "can this possibly be someone that I would be interested in spending the rest of my life with?" If you know within your heart that this person is not someone that you would want to begin a serious relationship with then don't waste your time or theirs. Your time is too precious and too valuable to spend on someone who God has not assigned or ordained for your life. While single, I limited myself in dating; I only dated someone that I felt might be my potential spouse. If I knew that he was not on my level, not saved or not ready for commitment, I did not waste my time nor did I jeopardize my anointing by getting involved in a relationship that was not edifying but would be a hindrance to my spiritual growth. I don't care how fine he is, how good he looks, or how expensive the car that he drives may be, if he is not saved, he is not dating material, he is a DANGER!

I remember, in my younger years, I remember one morning, I stopped at a known breakfast spot before going to work and as I walked in, there was a very attractive young man standing in line that seemed to be mesmerized by me as I walked in the door. He had a stare that he could not break; it was like I was a breath of fresh air to him. I could not help but embrace his admiration of me, it made me feel beautiful. I had not experienced that type of attention from the opposite sex in a while and it felt good to be noticed and to feel wanted. I had been divorced for years and had just entered into my place of wholeness. I stood in line behind him and I could feel the mutual attraction between us, he became nervous and uneasy with me standing behind him but he was too afraid to say anything to me. Therefore, he left out of the store without saying a word but after I had paid for my food and walked out of the store, he was waiting outside and he introduced himself to me and asked did I have a man. Well me with my sanctified self had been out of the dating game for so long, the first thing that came out of my mouth was yes the Lord!! He immediately said, that is the best man to have and he asked me for my telephone number, I told him no, but I said, "you can give me yours and I will call you". I have always had a rule, not to give a stranger my home phone number. I also never call a man on the first day that I get his telephone number, it makes you seem too anxious and to available. Therefore, I waited a few days before I called him and when I finally called, as we talked, I found out that he was not saved, he believed in God but he had not confessed God as His personal savior. I tried to justify that and say, well he knows church and acknowledges God, I can give him a chance but as I continued to have conversations with this man, his conversations would always end up on sex.

I made the mistake of telling him how long I had been celibate thinking that if I told him what I stood for he would respect that and not try me but to an unsaved man your celibacy sometimes can become a challenge to them. *Amos 3:3* says, *"How can two walk together except they agree"*. I found myself falling in lust, wondering what he was like in the bed and how he would make me feel. You see, he told me everything that my flesh wanted to hear and the temptation began to set in. This was becoming an unhealthy relationship and I had to make a conscious decision to end it or end up between the sheets. I chose to end it, my spiritual life was at stake and my anointing was too valuable to lose over a few minutes of lustful pleasure that would have left me with an unhealthy soul tie and STILL single.

Later, he confessed to me that he had told his friend guy that he was going to do everything in his power to cause me to have sex with him. It turned him on that I had been celibate for so long and that became a power serge for him. He told me that he had planned to pull out all his mac daddy skills and cause me to fall but in the process of him thinking of how to weaken me, the Lord spoke to him and said "touch not my Anointed and do my Prophet no harm". You see, Jesus had prayed for me that my faith fail me not. Thank God for my Heavenly Father that watches over me and Jesus Christ who intercedes on my behalf! When I am weak, He is made strong in my life!

I placed myself in a vulnerable position entering into a relationship with an unsaved man. We must understand that we cannot save anyone, only God can! Our emotions can lead us to someone God never intended for us; that's why it is vital that we walk after the spirit and not fulfill the lust of our flesh. If you choose to date someone not saved or who has another belief, you are in error to the Word of God. The bible tells us not to be unequally yoked with unbelievers in *2 Corinthians 6:14.* At the point you discover he does not acknowledge Jesus Christ as Lord, the most you can be is friends. Likewise, the moment he tells you he can't be in a monogamous relationship without having sex, it's time to move or you will soon find yourself compromising your Christian beliefs.

There are many clouds of witnesses in the Bible who allowed their flesh to get in the way when it came to companionship. It was the women that Solomon chose who turned his heart away from God.

1 Kings 11:1-6 NIV King Solomon, however, loved many foreign women besides Pharaoh's daughter—Moabites, Ammonites, Edomites, Sidonians and Hittites. ²They were from nations about which the LORD had told the Israelites, "You must not intermarry with them, because they will surely turn your hearts after their gods." Nevertheless, Solomon held fast to them in love. ³He had seven hundred wives of royal birth and three hundred concubines, and his wives led him astray. ⁴As Solomon grew old, his wives turned his heart after other gods, and his heart was not fully devoted to the LORD his God, as the heart of David his father had been. ⁵He followed Ashtoreth the goddess of the Sidonians, and Molek the detestable god of the Ammonites. ⁶So Solomon did evil in the eyes of the LORD; he did not follow the LORD completely, as David his father had done.

Solomon had two problems, (1) He loved many foreign women: Women who worshipped other gods and brought pagan influences to Israel. (2) He loved **many** women, rejecting God's plan from the beginning for one man and one woman to become one flesh in marriage (Matthew 19:4-6, Genesis 2:23-24). Solomon did what many of us have done. He somehow thought that he could change them or he would be the exception, that he would escape the consequences of this sin. His sin not only hurt him and his relationship with God but it also affected others. However, he learned the hard way that he was not the exception to this rule.

In dating, we must be careful that we do not want romance and sensual fulfillment more than we want the Lord. With all the wisdom that Solomon possessed, he was snared by the power of romantic and sensual love and it blinded him to the Word of God. The bible says…..he held fast to them in love, *1 Kings 11:2*, instead of giving them up to the Lord. There is an old saying "You are known by the company you keep", however, we also tend to become like the company we keep that is why we cannot be unequally yoked up together with someone who does not have the same values and morals as we have. (1 Corinthians 15:33).

Chapter 7

RULES & GUIDELINES TO DATING

1 Corinthians 14:40
Let all things be done decently and in order.

There are rules and guidelines in dating and as Christians, we must abide by them. The bible says "let all things be done decently and in order"...*1 Cor. 14:40*. God has an order to everything and in order to receive the blessings and favor of the Lord, we must do things His way and not the world's way or our way.

RULES TO DATING:

1. **Set Boundaries**. Determine the standards by which you choose to live and set boundaries around them. Do not alter them for the convenience of pleasing your flesh or for another. Make a vow to remain celibate until holy matrimony and if he can't abide by this rule, he is not for you.

2. **Guard Your Heart.** Above all else, guard your heart, for it is the wellspring of life (Proverbs 4:23). We must be careful that we do not allow our affections and

emotions get involved prematurely while dating. Be careful that you are not falling in lust or the ideal of being in love verses falling in love with that person for real.

3. **Date with Purpose in Mind.** If it is your desire to be married, then you should be dating with the purpose of trying to determine if that person would be a suitable husband for you. Use your dating experience to get to know him, his character, temperament, and behavior. Also, get to know his relationship with the Lord and his leadership abilities that would qualify him as a good husband. Remember Christians do not date as the world does. Casual dating can cause you to fall into a sex trap! Keep your guards up and date with PURPOSE in mind.

4. **Rate the place WHERE you date.** Sometimes being in the wrong place will influence you to do the wrong thing. Therefore, make sure you are going to the right kind of place when you go on a date.

5. **Date only other Christians.** Do not be yoked together with unbelievers. For what do righteousness and wickedness

have in common? Or what fellowship can light have with darkness? (2Corinthians 6:14). We often take this verse too likely but by taking heed, it will save you from a lot of heartache and wasted time. As you are grounded in your faith, so are others and thinking that you can change them is deception, only God can.

6. **Seek Counsel and Accountability**. If the relationship is getting serious, seek the wise counsel of your Pastor or spiritual mentor. They are not emotionally tied to the person you are dating and can see things that perhaps you cannot and give you some wise advice. Also, they ask questions you may be afraid to ask or even think to ask. In some instances, you may not like what your Pastor or Spiritual Mentor may say but they have your best interest in heart and will only give wisdom to help you and not hurt you.

Ask Yourself These Questions During The Dating Process:

- Do you have the same beliefs?
- Do you come from the same denomination, if not will your different beliefs be a hindrance to the relationship? Does he believe in speaking in tongues?
- If you are a woman minister, does he believe in women preachers? Will he accept your calling and can he handle your leadership role?
- What is his motive is he seeking a wife or a girlfriend.
- If you have children from a previous marriage or relationship, will he be able to love and accept your children as his own?
- Has he shown any signs of taking this relationship any further or are you in a fantasy zone?
- Does he stimulate your intellect?
- Are you attracting the wrong type of person? Make sure you are sending the right message in order to attract the right person.
- Have you introduced him to your Pastor for reinforcement, discernment and prayer?
- How do I know if he might be the one? Is it love or lust? 1 Corinthians 13:4-7

defines real love, so ask yourself the following questions:
- a. Are you patient with each other?
- b. Are you kind to each other?
- c. Are you ever envious of each other?
- d. Do you never boast to or about each other?
- e. Is your relationship characterized by humility?
- f. Are you ever rude to each other?
- g. Are you easily angered with one another?
- h. Do you keep record of each other's wrongs?
- i. Are you truthful with each other?
- j. Do you protect each other?
- k. Do you trust each other?

Chapter 8

WHILE YOU'RE WAITING

Isaiah 40:31
³¹ But they that wait upon the LORD shall renew their strength; they shall mount up with wings as eagles; they shall run, and not be weary; and they shall walk, and not faint.

Many of us are not good at waiting for anything but yet we know that the best things come to those who patiently wait on the Lord. We, as Christians, must learn patience because it is patience that helps shapes our Christian character and increases our faith. As we yield to the Holy Spirit, He is the one that produces "the fruit of the Spirit" on the inside of us.

The *Greek word* primarily used for patience in the KJV is **"hypomone"**, and it means *"cheerful (or hopeful) endurance, constancy: - enduring, patience, patient continuance (waiting)."* While waiting on God to bless you with a spouse, you must maintain the right spirit. Many women tend to look at others who are getting married and become disgruntled, discouraged and even bitter because it's not them getting married. This is the wrong spirit and attitude to have. The bible tells us to rejoice with those that rejoice. We must be happy when we see others being blessed, so when it's your time others will rejoice with you. In Psalms, David said, "I will bless the Lord at all times. His praise shall continually be in my mouth." At all times mean when He gives me the answer to my prayer as well as while I am waiting on Him to manifest the answer to my prayers.

For the joy of the Lord is your strength, (Nehemiah 8:10).

Your attitude while waiting plays a major role in the releasing of your blessings. Sometimes, you can hinder the Lord's blessings from being released to you because you have the wrong spirit. *Habakkuk 2:4 says "Behold, his soul which is lifted up is not upright in him: but the just shall live by his faith."* Your negative attitude displays that you have a lack of faith in what God promised you. When you have a good attitude, you keep yourself strong and optimistic to the will of God for your life. That positive attitude of faith will open the way for God to work miracles in your life and release blessings! While waiting on God, meditate on the goodness and promises of God and be full of His joy!

Webster's dictionary defines patience as "*The suffering of afflictions, pain, toil, calamity, provocation or other evil, with a calm, unruffled temper; endurance without murmuring or fretfulness. Patience may spring from constitutional fortitude, from a kind of heroic pride,* **or from Christian submission to the divine will.** *A calm temper which bears evils without murmuring or discontent.*" Meaning that you will not always feel good while waiting. Temptations will arise and doubt will try to creep in and make you think that you are unwanted, undesirable and unlovable. But you must stand strong during your time of adversity and know that God has not forgotten you. Ephesians 6:13 says "Put on the full armor of God, so that when the day of evil comes, you may be able to stand your ground." Patience will birth out stability and long suffering in you. You must adapt to a mindset that if I never get married, I will still serve the Lord with gladness!

Sometimes, when you least expect it, is when God bless you. In other words, it's when you get your mind and affection off of "it" (being married) and on God and the things of God. Women, there are so many things that you can accomplish and achieve while being single.

While you are waiting on God to bless you with a husband, ladies what are you doing with your Time; Yourself and your Money?

TIME: Your time is valuable and once time passes you cannot get it back. Many single women waste time by fantasying about what Mr. Wright will be like and/or what their house and children will look like; but, what does all that accomplish? Absolutely nothing! It's good to dream but don't get caught up in fantasying all day long, every day, and find yourself unproductive. A "blessed" man prospers in everything that he does because he has learned to flow with the seasons that have been uniquely designed for his life, instead of working against them.

Time is your best friend when used appropriately. While you are single, use time to your advantage by doing things that will prosper your life. Do things that will make you prosper in the earth and cause you to leave a great legacy behind. So many times women wait for a mate in order to accomplish certain dreams and to do great exploits. A man does not make you great, God does. The man only adds to your value. Now, as a single woman, is the time to build your own empire!

YOURSELF: Is your house in order? When is the last time you took an inventory of yourself? While waiting on God, focus on you, becoming the best that you can possible be. This is the time to educate yourself, obtain your college degree or certificate in a trade. Once you become married, your time becomes more limited. It's never too late to return to school or accomplish your goals.

Sometimes, we think we are ready for certain things when in actuality we need to work on us some more. Women, once you become married and you and your spouse are living as one, you can't do house chores when you feel like it. Men like a clean and organized environment or he can become easily frustrated. In my many years of marriage counseling, one of the primary complaints that I received from the husband was that his wife did not clean up the house. So, while waiting, practice doing laundry, cooking and cleaning on a regular basis. Preparation sets you up for success and develops discipline in you. Therefore, once you are married, you are already use to doing these things consistently. These things may seem small and irrelevant to you but I have seen many married couples in an uproar because of these things and some even headed to divorce court.

What about your health? Are you healthy and in good shape? This is a perfect time to work on these important areas in your life while being single. You want to be healthy and strong so you can be vibrant in your marriage.

MONEY. Do you have some and do you know how to manage it? This is crucial when you believe God to soon enter into a marriage. Mismanaging and a lack of money is one of the leading causes of divorce. Yes, the man is considered the head of the home and has the responsibility to be able to provide for his family but sisters, we are also his helpmate and not this debt mate. While you are single, learn how to make and manage your money. Watch how you spend and what you spend it on. Your money should have a purpose! When a famer plants seed into the ground, he knows the name of that seed, so he can know what type of harvest he can expect to grow! You must sow where you intend to grow and go! When a farmer sows a seed he knows not to expect a harvest the next day but he is sure to cultivate that ground and keep looking for a harvest to eventually spring up!

We can learn so much wisdom from the virtuous woman in Proverbs 31. She not only found favor in the sight of God but also in the heart and eyes of her husband. She knew how to make and manage money to add increase and provision to her household. She did not keep her husband in debt because she was busy shopping at Nordstrom's every day. As a matter of fact, she had many virtues that we can glean from.

1. **Proverbs 31:13** - She seeth wool, and flax, and worketh willingly with her hands. She had a skill; she knew how to sew and make clothes for her family and kept them well dressed for the weather and for the occasion.
2. **Proverbs 31:14** - She is like the merchants' ships; she bringeth her food from afar. This sister knew how to cook, she learned new recipes so her husband would not get tired of eating the same old thing.
3. **Proverbs 31:15** - She riseth also while it is yet night, and giveth meat to her household, and a portion to her maidens. She was not a lazy woman who slept all day but she got up early before the sun rose and fed her family. Women that man does not want fast food but a home cooked food like his momma use to cook!

4. **Proverbs 31:16** - She considereth a field, and buyeth it: with the fruit of her hands she planteth a vineyard. She was a business woman and knew how to make financial transactions and decisions. She was knowledgeable, wise and ambitious.
5. **Proverbs 31:17** - She girdeth her loins with strength, and strengtheneth her arms. She had balance, while taking care of her household, she yet took care of herself!

Lastly women, what is your credit score? We want a man that has it all together but that man also wants a woman that has it all together. We know that no one will be perfect or have everything just right but we can have our basics down! Make sure your credit score is decent and above average. Entering into a marriage, you don't want to be the one that causes the house loan to be denied or have your name omitted from the mortgage because of your credit. Your credit reveals your stewardship and how you take care of your responsibilities.

It is my earnest prayer Daughter of Abraham that you become whole and complete in Christ before you commit to marriage. When your Boaz finds you, may he find you gleaning (garnering, gathering, collecting and assembling). What God has for you it is for you!

A LIST OF DEFINITIONS

All definitions are taken from Webster, Merriam-Webster or Wikipedia.

ADULTERY – Voluntary sexual intercourse between a married person and a person who is not his or her spouse.

CELIBATE - (from Latin, *cælibatus"*) is the state of voluntarily being unmarried, sexually abstinent, or both, usually for religious reasons.

BOYFRIEND - 1: a male friend. 2: a frequent or regular male companion in a romantic or sexual relationship.

DESIRE - **Desire**, wish, want, crave, covet mean to have a longing for. **Desire** stresses the strength of feeling and often implies strong intention or aim.

FORNICATION - Sexual intercourse between people not married to each other.

FRIENDSHIP - The state of being friends: the relationship between friends. A friendly feeling or attitude: kindness or help given to someone.

GIRLFRIEND - A woman that someone is having a romantic or sexual relationship with. : A female friend.

HOLY - Set apart for the service of God or of a divine being.

LOVE – A profoundly tender, passionate affection for another person. 2. a feeling of warm personal attachment or deep affection, as for a parent, child, or friend. 3. Sexual passion or desire.

LUST – A strong feeling of sexual desire. : a strong desire for something.

MARRIED - the state of being united to a person of the opposite sex as husband or wife in a consensual and contractual relationship recognized by law.

RESPECT - A feeling of admiring someone or something that is good, valuable, important, etc.: a feeling or understanding that someone or something is important, serious, etc., and should be treated in an appropriate way. A particular way of thinking about or looking at something.

SEX - physical activity in which people touch each other's bodies, kiss each other, etc.:

physical activity that is related to and often includes **sexual** intercourse.

SINGLE - *1a*: not married *b*: of or relating to celibacy; consisting of a separate unique whole individual.

STANDARD - A level of quality, achievement, etc., that is considered acceptable or desirable. **Standards**: ideas about morally correct and acceptable behavior. Something that is very good and that is used to make judgments about the quality of other things.

TEMPTATION - A strong urge or desire to have or do something. Something that causes a strong urge or desire to have or do something and especially something that is bad, wrong, or unwise.

VIRGIN - A **virgin** is someone who has never had sex.

WHOLE - **1**. all of; entire. **2**. in an unbroken or undamaged state; in one piece. *noun*: **the whole** a thing that is complete in itself.